Wynne - A -

21 Days to a new way of thinking

<u>Preface:</u>

Phenomenal Day Family! I am a firm believer that "how you start your day determines the rest of it". Make a decision to choose to start your day with me for the next 21 days straight.

In order to have change, you need to face challenges. In the word challenge, you will find the word change. So I challenge you to follow the rules of this book. Are you ready?

Rule #1: read only 1 page per day & allow it to soak in for 24hrs
Rule #2: read for 21 days straight, No Breaks In-between
Rule #3: If you miss a day, you have to start over from day 1.

It takes an eternity to eliminate a bad habit. It takes only 21 days to develop a habit. So the best thing is creating good habits that will eventually take the place of bad habits. The key to this book is creating good habits. Habits: a usual way of behaving : something that a person does often in a regular and repeated way.

Let's be intentional with our actions. Consistent action leads to habits. Good habits leads to great outcomes. Great outcomes results in true happiness. I believe you will abide by the rules because you seek the happiness which will come from the change in this book. Now let's get to it.

<u>Day 1:</u>

Great Day Family. You are going somewhere that most people cannot. In order to get there, you must not be submerged in a person's perspective, that's not on the level in which you are going. Separate from them and adjust your attitude. Change your mindset so you can flow through the process.
#GetWynneInspired

<u>Day 2:</u>

Phenomenal Day Family. Often times we get stuck in a cycle that mentally we think cannot change. The only cycle you cannot change is the cycle of seasons. Winter, then spring, then summer, then fall, then winter again. The faster you realize this, the sooner you will understand how powerful you are. So first, identify what season you are in. Second, act accordingly and immediately. Third, in the process understand you have what it takes to change. You must want change and it starts from within. Lastly repeat step 1.

#GetWynneInspired

<u>Day 3:</u>

Phenomenal Day Family. Diamonds are made from extreme heat and pressure. The diamond becomes of high value because of the process it went through. Whether you are going in, currently in, or coming out of the process, the result makes you extremely valuable.
#GetWynneInspired

<u>Day 4:</u>

Great Day Family. "You learn how bright the light is only in darkness". Appreciate those DARK moments because you were set up to SUCCEED and CONQUER . Watch what happens in the DARK. Pay attention to your LIGHT!!!

#GetWynneInspired

<u>Day 5:</u>

What if losing it all was supposed to happen. It was needed for you to shift your mindset. So that when you do gain, it is more this time than what you had before. When it is the same amount, yet it feels like more because of a change in perspective. So! Look at it differently. Have a Phenomenal Day Family

#GetWynneInspired

<u>Day 6:</u>

Great Day Family. Have thoughts ever cross your mind as to why there are so many trials and tribulation that you must go through in a current season of change? The major reason is that there is a greater prize once you push through. There is a next level coming, a great blessing. So the opposition places you in position to receive it.

#GetWynneInspired

<u>Day 7:</u>

Great Day Family. You have extremely high value. Because of that, your very being is needed. Share some of your value today. Whether it is a conversation, your presence, or just an act. SHARE YOUR VALUE
#GetWynneInspired

<u>Day 8:</u>

Phenomenal Day Family. Sometimes our biggest challenge is who we are up against. Which is the ENEMY. Constantly going to battle with the opponent yet unclear of who it really is. Well, in fact, it starts within us. Who your actually going up against is your inner - me. You can get into your own head and stop your own blessings. The solution is to feed your subconscious mind. It is about time that you get into your head intentionally. Change the things that you see and hear everyday. Only set it on positive affirmations, personal goals, desires and the word of GOD. Only then will change come from the challenge.

#GetWynneInspired

<u>Day 9:</u>

Phenomenal Day Family. Sometimes starting over does not mean completely start over. Sometimes it means to start again. This year is not about new year new me. Its about new year, better me. Dont throw away your progress. Make the most of it and you will receive the best because of it.

#GetWynneInspired

11

__Day 10:__

Phenomenal Day Family. What are you speaking over your life? What you speak, you hear. What you hear, your subconscious believes. What your subconscious believes, becomes your reality. Speak highly of yourself. Here are some affirmations: I Am Powerful. I Am More Than Enough. I am Able to do all things in Christ. I am loveds. I am full of results. I am grateful for all that I have. I am a leader. I am full of opportunities that creates wealth. I am creative. I am gifted. I am Phenomenal.

#GetWynneInspired

<u>Day 11:</u>

The power of FREE! It is more effective on the giver than the receiver. When you give freely, you do it completely without expectation of a good reaction. Now, what your doing has unlimited power and effect. When you want to receive free things, you lose the value of what it is. Because if you get challenged to fight for it or lose it, you would be quick to give it up. It was 0 risk to gain it, so its nothing to lose. "You Value and honor what you pay for". So, I ask of you to do 2 things. Pay ATTENTION. INVEST in YOUR FUTURE. Have a PHENOMENAL DAY FAMILY.
#GetWynneInspired

13

<u>Day 12:</u>

Phenomenal Day Family. Extreme Focus: Creating a tunnel vision where all you see is your goal. A goal is simply a dream with a date attached to it. What is that dream and when do you want to accomplish it. ALlow yourself to gain a clear sight as to what you want, where you want to be, and who you will become.

#GetWynneInspired

<u>Day 13:</u>

Phenomenal Day Family. What is your WHY? This will be repeated over and over until we get it. Sometimes we minimize our WHY just to say we have one. Your WHY is personal because its about people you care for the most. Your WHY got to hurt you in way that pushes you to make it happen! If your WHY does not make you emotional, then revamp it. Remember who you do it for!

#GetWynneInspired

15

<u>Day 14:</u>

It is a Phenomenal Day Family. Often times we ask the question "why are we going through the things that we go through"? The fact of the matter is that the more things you go through, the closer you are to who you need to become. It is always too early to quit. There is a process you need to get through to get to your purpose. The only way through is through. S conquer that situation. Repeat after me... I REFUSE TO LOSE!

#GetWynneInspired

<u>Day 15:</u>

Phenomenal Day Family. Sometimes all the closure you need about a situation is to realize it is closed. The focus should be on your future, not what could have worked out. Whatyou need are things that are absolutely going to work in your favor. You are promised so much more. Let go of what was and embrace what is and who you are going to be. And that is Phenomenal!!!
#GetWynneInspired

<u>Day 16:</u>

Phenomenal Day Family. What if you saw exactly how you affect people? What if you failing, helps someone succeed? What if taking less now, meant more very soon? What if taking the risk this time, really works? Based on your answers, you are saying through the process, its worth it. So, I ask of you, GET THROUGH IT!!!
#GetWynneInspired

18

<u>Day 17:</u>

Phenomenal Day Family. GOD allowed a word to be formed, "IMPOSSIBLE". He did that to send you a message, that all things through him is possible . Most importantly he used that as an echo. Because if he created us in his image, and called us to have power in his likeness, then you can as well. So, once you repeat these following words, HEAR GOD'S VOICE AND HEAR YOUR OWN. " IM POSSIBLE".

#GetWynneInspired

<u>Day 18:</u>

Phenomenal Day Family. Your greatest powers in SUCCESS comes from within your 5 senses. What you listen to constantly becomes your language (Ears). What you see is what makes your environment (Eyes). What you say becomes truth (Mouth). If you can feel it, you can have it (Touch). What you smell becomes your appetite (Nose). The ability of SUCCESS is already obtained by you.
#GetWynneInspired

Day 19:

The 2 requirements for going elite are CONSISTENCY and DISCIPLINE. You got to be CONSISTENTLY DISCIPLINED to provide DISCIPLINED results CONSISTENTLY. The only way to do that is practice CONSISTENCY so that everything is embedded in you because you stayed DISCIPLINE. Phenomenal Day Family.
#GetWynneInspired

<u>Day 20:</u>

Don't rush the process. The purpose for the process is to prepare you for the prize. It don't make sense to receive the reward and your not ready for it. Take action now. It doesnt matter how, just as long as you know you are going to #GetWynneInspired

<u>Day 21:</u>

Phenomenal Day Family. I just want to I say thank you for 2 things. 1 is participating in your growth. Being able to listen and apply what is brought to you. 2 is supporting my vision to help people in this way. I would not be who I am if it were not for you. You are my WHY. You are the reason I stay consistent . You are the best thing that has ever happened to me. And that is simply because you are PHENOMENAL!

#GetWynneInspired

<u>About the author:</u>

Ronald Wynne is the CEO, Founder and one of the hosts of "Your Perspective Matters" Podcast. Born in New York City. Specifically the bronx. Through the power of entrepreneurship, it has challenged his mindset allowing him to grow and live in multiple states like Houston, TX and Las Vegas, NV. With several years of entrepreneurship, it has lead Ronald down a path of focusing everything he do on personal growth. That's one of the big reasons this book was birthed from.

With personal development being his top priority in life, it pushes him to impact hundreds of people that crosses his path. Leveraging his gift of speaking and effective thinking, is where his purpose lies. No college degree, just faith and direction from GOD is where he builds his leagacy. You are apart of it too! So spread the word. Take this book seriously because someone's life depends on it. Help Ronald impact millions by creating a new habit.